Hi Girls!

Hey, scripture heroes are NOT just boys! The scriptures are full of great heroes that were **WOMEN** too! I've created this book with a few of my favorite heroines (that's a fancy name for a female hero ☺) from the Bible and Book of Mormon . . . **especially for you!** I hope you enjoy their stories and APPLY them to your own life.

Each hero has her own **SCRIPTURE POWER** verse(s) to go with her story. Practice saying these verses over and over 'til you have them memorized. Can you do that? Awesome! They are special scriptures that the prophet wants you to learn (sometimes called Scripture Mastery verses).

Also, when you get a little older, you will start going to Young Womens and will learn the eight **Young Women's VALUES.** So, let's get a headstart! ☺ At the end of the book, where the Family Home Evening Lesson Helps are, you will also learn a YW Value that goes with each heroine. Sweet!

Now, let's get to these great girl heroes!

EVE
Makes the
Best Choice, p. 1

GARDEN
OF
EDEN

HANNAH
Prays with Faith, p. 24

TABERNACLE

OLD TESTAMENT

OLD WORLD

JERUSALEM

REBEKAH
Loves Doing Good Works, p. 10

SARIAH
Obeys the Lord
Willingly, p. 34

4000 BC   1850 BC   1050 BC   600 BC

THE BOOK OF MORMON

NEW WORLD

ABISH
Acts on Inspiration, p. 62

ESTHER
Stands Up for the Right, p. 46

IN PERSIA

SWING

MARY
Lives a Virtuous Life, p.72

NEW TESTAMENT

BETHLEHEM

Family Home Evening Lesson Helps, p. 82

480 BC

90 BC

0 AD

EVE
Makes the Best Choice

Hello, my name is Eve.
I am the first daughter of our Heavenly Father to ever
live on the earth. That means we're related! I want to tell
you about the time I had to make a hard decision
and **choose the best choice.**

Scripture Power!

" . . . (we) are free to choose liberty and eternal life, through the
great Mediator of all men (Jesus Christ) . . . "— 2 Nephi 2:27

My husband, Adam, and I lived a long, long, loooooong time ago in a beautiful place called the Garden of Eden. Life was pretty easy. We had everything we needed and didn't have to work for anything. And our bodies were immortal—that means we did not get sick, get old, or die. However, while we were in the garden, we were not able to have children. (Moses 2:26-27, 3:15, 3:18, 21-24)

As Adam and I enjoyed the garden, we ate fruit from all the trees . . . except one. Heavenly Father told us that if we ate *that* fruit, things would change: We would have to leave the Garden of Eden; life would become much harder; and we would become mortal and die someday. But, we would be able to start our own family.

(Moses 3:16–17)

I had a tough choice to make! Should I eat the fruit or not? Staying in the Garden of Eden was the *easy* choice, but was it the *best* choice? Heavenly Father had commanded Adam and me to have children, and we could only do that if we ate the fruit and became mortal. *What was most important?* I wondered. I decided to eat the fruit, and Adam did too.

Moses 2:28, 4:12)

3

The rest of our lives was difficult, but it was worth it! After leaving Eden, Adam and I learned to appreciate the good because life was no longer easy all the time. Best of all, we discovered the joy of having a family! And, we learned of our Savior who would make it possible for all of us to return and live with Heavenly Father after we died. I knew I had **made the best choice!** (Moses 5:1-2, 5:9-12)

How can you MAKE THE BEST CHOICE like Eve?

" . . . (we) are free to choose liberty and eternal life, through the great Mediator of all men (Jesus Christ) . . . "— 2 Nephi 2:27

5

Your life is full of choices! Using your agency to make right choices is an important part of growing up. But sometimes it's hard to choose.

Think about the consequences of your choice. How will you feel *afterwards?* Some choices might seem fun or easy at the moment, but which choice will bring you the most happiness in the long run?

Follow the Spirit. The peaceful, calm feeling of the spirit will let you know what you should do. It may take more effort to follow those promptings, but it's always worth it.

Making the best choices, even when it's tough, is what this life is all about. It strengthens your character (ask your parents what that means ☺). Remember what President Monson says:

"Decisions Determine Destiny!" (April 2002 Gen. Conf.)

REBEKAH
Loves Doing Good Works

Hi there! I'm Rebekah.
Do you love to **do good works?** I sure do. I want to tell you about a good deed I did for someone else and was greatly blessed for it.

Scripture Power!

". . . (we) should be anxiously engaged in a good cause, and do many things of (our) own free will, and bring to pass much righteousness" — D&C 58:27

One evening, I went to the well to get water for my family. That was my responsibility, and I was happy to do it.

After I had filled my water pitcher, a man suddenly came up to me and asked if he could have a drink. I could tell he had traveled a long way and was thirsty, so I gladly gave him some of my water.

(Genesis 24:17-18)

Then I noticed that he had ten camels with him. *They sure look thirsty too,* I thought. So I told the man that I would draw water for all his camels as well.

(Genesis 24:19)

And, let me tell you, camels can drink **A LOT** of water!! I went back and forth from the well many, many times. Finally, all the camels were full . . . and I was EXHAUSTED! Even though I was tired, it felt good helping someone who needed help.

(Genesis 24:20-21)

Later that evening, my parents welcomed the man into our home and invited him to have dinner with us. As we sat down to eat, the man said he had something very important to tell us.

(Genesis 24:23-25, 31, 33)

15

He said that he was a servant of the prophet, Abraham. He had been sent to our land to find a wife with righteous qualities for Abraham's son, Isaac. While he and his camels were resting at the well, he watched the young women of the town coming out to get water. *Could one of these young women be the right one to marry Isaac?* he wondered. **Hhhmmmm.**

(Genesis 24:34-38)

Suddenly, he had an idea! He prayed and asked the Lord to let the right young woman be the one who gives him something to drink *and* . . . offers to give water to all of his camels as well. When he said that, I was shocked! That was exactly what I had done! The Holy Ghost then prompted me that I should go with him and meet Isaac.

(Genesis 24:42-46, 49, 57-58)

17

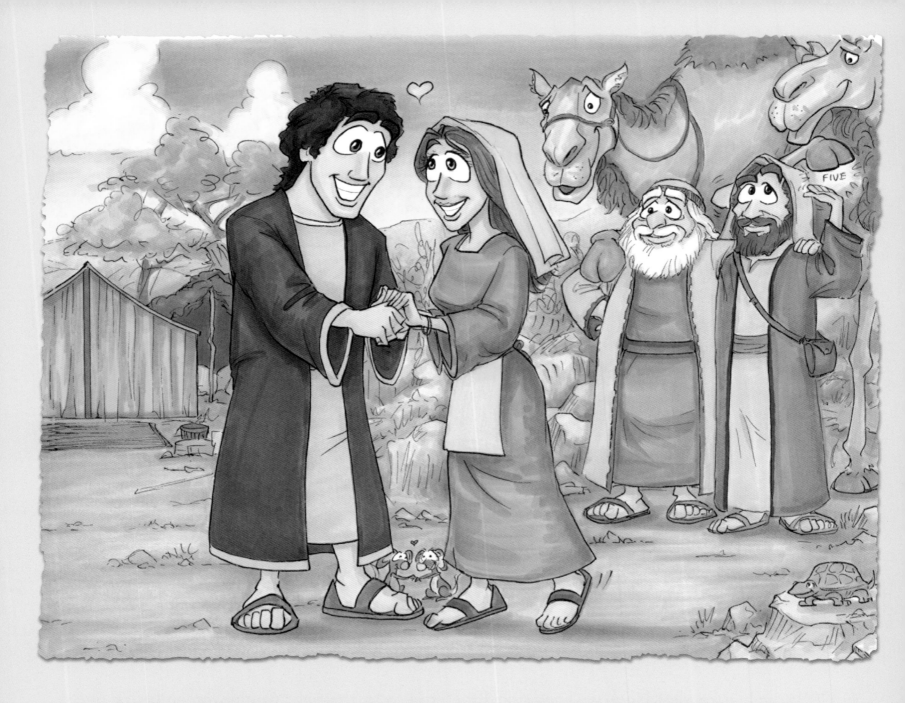

I returned with Abraham's servant to his land and was married to Isaac. We had a happy life together and received many blessings from the Lord. I knew Heavenly Father had blessed me because of the righteous qualities that I had developed while I was young. (Genesis 24:61-67)

How can you LOVE DOING GOOD WORKS like Rebekah?

". . . (we) should be anxiously engaged in a good cause, and do many things of (our) own free will, and bring to pass much righteousness"— D&C 58:27

Jesus taught that serving others is one of the best good works you can do. So when others ask for help, **be happy to serve** them.

Its even MORE fun to **serve people when they DON'T ask for help.** Always be on the lookout for other's needs. Become a "good works detective!"

Go the extra mile! See what *more* you can do in your good works. Go beyond what is expected. It feels good when you do your best to serve someone. And then . . .

Be sure to **enjoy that good, tired feeling after you're done.** And who knows what blessings Heavenly Father has in store for *you* . . . as you develop the righteous quality of doing good works?

23

HANNAH
Prays with Faith

Greetings, my
young friends. My name is Hannah.
In my life, I learned that when we **pray with faith,**
Heavenly Father will hear and answer our prayers.
Let me tell you how I learned that lesson.

Scripture Power!

". . . faith is things which are hoped for and not seen . . . ye
receive no witness until after the trial of your faith."— Ether 12:6

More than anything, I wanted to be a mother. However, after many years of being married, I did not have any children. I was so sad! My kind husband tried to comfort me, but it didn't help. What could I do? I decided to **pray in faith** to my Heavenly Father and ask Him to bless me with a child.

(1 Samuel 1:2, 5-8)   25

One day, I went to the temple to pray for this blessing. I knelt down and pleaded with the Lord. I promised that if He would let me have a child, "then I (would) give him unto the Lord all the days of his life."

(1 Samuel 1:9-11)

A priest at the temple named Eli heard me praying. He told me that Heavenly Father had heard my prayer and would bless me with a baby.

(1 Samuel 1:12, 17-18)

I was so **happy!** And sure enough, sometime later, I had a baby boy! Now I knew the Lord had all power to bless us when we **pray in faith.** I named the boy Samuel.

(1 Samuel 1:19-20)

As Samuel grew older, I knew that I had to keep my promise to the Lord. So, I returned to the temple to show my son to Eli. I asked Eli if Samuel could live with him at the temple and learn how to serve the Lord. It was hard to let him go, but I knew it was the right thing to do and that I would be blessed again for my sacrifice.

(1 Samuel 1:24-28)

And I was blessed! As the years went by, my husband and I had several more children. And Samuel grew into a righteous young man who later became one of God's prophets. I knew that I had received all these blessings because of my **faithful prayers.** Thank you, Heavenly Father!

(1 Samuel 2:20-21, 3:19-20)

How can you PRAY WITH FAITH like Hannah?

". . . faith is things which are hoped for and not seen . . . ye receive no witness until after the trial of your faith."— Ether 12:6

Heavenly Father loves you and is anxious to answer your prayers. **Have a righteous desire** in your heart when you ask for His blessings. Kneel down and pray out loud. **Ask in faith,** believing that your prayers will be answered.

SOMETIME LATER

Heavenly Father hears and **answers faithful prayers . . . but in His own time and way.** Always trust that He knows what is best for you. Oh, and don't forget to give back to the Lord by sacrificing for Him. That is the best way to **show your gratitude!**

33

SARIAH
Obeys the Lord
Willingly

Hello, my young friends.
My name is Sariah. I want to tell you
about the journey our family made to the Promised
Land. What an adventure that was! During our travels,
I learned that we should always **obey the Lord
willingly,** even when it's hard.

Scripture Power!

"Trust in the Lord with all thine heart . . . and he shall direct
thy paths." —Proverbs 3:5–6

One day, the Lord commanded our family to leave our home in Jerusalem and go live in the wilderness. Nobody really *wanted* to leave. We enjoyed our home and our belongings in Jerusalem. But we knew it was a commandment from the Lord, so we trusted in Him and obeyed.

(1 Nephi 2:1-4)

A few days after we left, the Lord commanded our sons to go back to Jerusalem and get the plates of brass from Laban. I knew how difficult and dangerous that would be; Laban was a very wicked man. But my sons did as they were commanded and returned to the city. I trusted that the Lord would take care of them.

(1 Nephi 3:1-4, 7-9)

But, oh how I worried! When they didn't come back after a while, I feared something terrible had happened to them. *Was the Lord **really** protecting my sons from Laban?* I cried. We moms have a right to worry about our kids! I am thankful for my husband who comforted me during this hard time.

(1 Nephi 5:2-6)

At last, my boys returned! **Yeah!** I was one happy mom! ☺ And they had succeeded in getting the plates of brass from Laban. Now I *knew* that Heavenly Father was watching over us and protecting us. Our family had obeyed His commandment—even when it was difficult—and had been blessed for it.

(1 Nephi 4:1, 5:1, 7-9)

For many years we journeyed through the barren wilderness. We lived in tents. We hunted for our food. We suffered many hardships. We built a ship to take us to the Promised Land, just as the Lord had commanded us. None of this was easy, but we still obeyed.

(1 Nephi 16:15-17, 17:1, 4, 8, 15)

Eventually, we arrived in the Promised Land! **Hooray!** In the end, I saw that our journey had been a test: *Who would obey God's commandments with the right attitude?* Sadly, some in our group whined and complained a lot. But, many of us **obeyed the Lord willingly** with little complaint . . . and so can you! *That* kind of obedience brings blessings.

(1 Nephi 18:22-23, 2 Nephi 1:1-5)

How can you OBEY THE LORD WILLINGLY like Sariah?

"Trust in the Lord with all thine heart . . . and he shall direct thy paths."
—Proverbs 3:5–6

Sometimes, keeping God's commandments means we have to sacrifice or give up something we want. **Obey** anyway! **Even if you don't feel like it.** Trust that Heavenly Father knows what is best for you.

Have faith to **do what God asks . . . especially when it's hard!** You can be sure that . . .

43

. . . **G**od will help you do what He commands.

He prepares a way for you to obey!

Obey with the right attitude. Bad attitude obedience doesn't do anyone much good.

45

ESTHER
Stands Up for the Right

Hi there, girls.
My name is Esther.
Have you ever had to **stand up for what is right?**
It takes courage, doesn't it? Let me tell you my
experience with that.

Scripture Power!

"I can do all things through Christ which strengtheneth me."
— Philippians 4:13

I was raised by my adopted father, Mordecai. We were Jews living in a faraway land. We believed in God. However, most of the people around us were not Jewish and did not believe in God.

(Esther 2:5-7)

One day, an announcement was made that the king was looking for a new queen. Many young women went to the palace in hopes that the king would choose them to be his queen. I was one of them. However, I told no one that I was Jewish.

48

(Esther 2:2, 4, 8, 10)

We stayed at the king's palace for many months. Each of us had a chance to meet the king. Finally, the king chose one of us to be his wife. It was **me!** I couldn't believe it. We married and I became his queen.

(Esther 2:15-17) 49

Meanwhile, the king had an advisor named Haman. He was a wicked man who hated the Jews. Haman tricked the king into believing that all the Jews were dangerous and that they should be killed. The king gave Haman permission to do this terrible thing!

(Esther 3:1, 8-11, 13)

When I learned about this, I was so worried! I was a Jew too! I wanted to save my people, but I was scared to talk to the king. He had been in the inner court for many days. There was a law that said—*Anyone who enters the king's inner court without being invited would be killed. However, if the king holds out his golden scepter, he or she will be allowed to speak.*   (Esther 4:4, 8, 11)

51

As I was worrying, I received a letter from Mordecai that gave me courage. He told me that perhaps the Lord had blessed me to become the queen *"for such a time as this"* . . . so that I could save my people. I knew I needed to have faith and **stand up for what was right.**

(Esther 4:13-14)

The day came to go into the inner court and see the king. I had been praying and fasting that the Lord would help me. All the Jews were fasting for me as well. *Here goes,* I thought . . .

(Esther 4:15-17)

"What would you like, Queen Esther?" asked the king.

"I want to invite you and Haman to a banquet that I have prepared," I replied.

(Esther 5:1-4)

The next night, at the banquet, I told the king the truth. I told him that I was a Jew. I told him that my people were not dangerous and that Haman was his enemy, not the Jews. The king believed me. He was angry at Haman for lying to him and had *him* killed, instead of all of my people.

(Esther 7:1-6, 9-10)

With the Lord's help, I had saved my people. I was so relieved. And the king chose my father, Mordecai, to take Haman's place as his new advisor. I was glad that I had followed God's plan for my life and **stood up for the right.**

(Esther 8;1-2, 16-17)

How can you STAND UP FOR THE RIGHT like Esther?

 "I can do all things through Christ which strengtheneth me."
— Philippians 4:13

Just like Esther, YOU have been put on the earth "for such a time as this." Father in Heaven trusts you to **stand up for the right in every situation you are in**...even if it's difficult.

You can **gain courage through the support of family, friends, and church leaders.** They all believe in you and support you. Many of them pray for you on a regular basis.

59

Live **righteously** and do those things that will prepare you to stand for the right. Righteous living fills you with the Holy Ghost and gives you confidence when you need it!

Then, **do it!** Just as Esther didn't "chicken out" at the last minute . . . **when the moment comes to stand for the right, don't be afraid.** Don't worry what other people will think. What Heavenly Father thinks is all that matters.

61

ABISH
Acts on Inspiration

Welcome. I'm Abish.
Do you know what it means to receive inspiration?
It means to do something good when you are prompted
by the Holy Spirit. I want to tell you about a time when
I helped others believe in God because I **acted
on inspiration.**

Scripture Power!

". . . I will tell you in your mind and in your heart, by the Holy Ghost
. . . Now, behold, this is the spirit of revelation." — D&C 8:2-3

I was a servant to the Lamanite king and queen. A Nephite missionary named Ammon had been teaching the king about the Lord and His gospel. I already had a testimony of the gospel and was excited to see my king learning about it too. (Alma 18:36, 39)

One day, I went into the king's chambers and found the king, the queen, Ammon, and the other servants all on the ground as if they were dead. **Whoa!** But I knew they weren't actually dead. Instead, they had fallen down because the power of God was changing their hearts. *This gave me an idea . . .*

(Alma 19:16-17)

I ran from house to house, telling everyone what had just happened. I wanted them to come and see what the power of God had just done. I thought this might help them believe in God too.

(Alma 19:17)

However, when the people saw the scene, some were scared. Others were confused. Still, others were angry. Instead of seeing God's power and being happy, they began to argue with each other about what this meant.

(Alma 19:18-19, 25-27)

Oh, no! I had better do something, I cried. ***This gave me an idea . . .***

I reached down and took the queen's hand, hoping that she would wake up if I touched her. And guess what? She did wake up! **Phew.**

(Alma 19:28-29) 67

The queen stood up and began telling the people that the Lord had changed her heart. Then the king, Ammon, and the servants all stood up and began bearing their testimonies. The people felt the Spirit and began to believe in God as well. It was amazing! I was so glad that I had **acted on inspiration.**

(Alma 19:29-36)

How can you ACT ON INSPIRATION like Abish?

 ". . . I will tell you in your mind and in your heart, by the Holy Ghost . . .
Now, behold, this is the spirit of revelation."— D&C 8:2-3

Do YOU ever get ideas about ways you can help someone or about good things you can do? Those thoughts come from the Holy Ghost! It's called receiving inspiration. **Always pay attention to those ideas** and then . . .

. . . **A**CT on them! Do those good deeds, even if they seem unusual or if no one else is doing it. Those small, simple ideas can help great things to happen.

MARY
Lives a Virtuous Life

Hello, girls. My name is Mary. I was chosen to be the mother of the Savior, Jesus Christ. What a holy privilege that was! Here's my story.

Scripture Power!

"And ye must practice virtue and holiness before me continually."—D&C 46:33

I was a young woman living in a city called Nazareth. While growing up, I had always done my best to obey God's commandments and **live a virtuous life.** Now, I was engaged to be married to a righteous man named Joseph.

One day, a most wonderful thing happened! An angel of the Lord appeared to me. He told me that I was "highly favored" by God and that I was "blessed among women." He then said that because of my virtue, I would be the mother of the Son of God. His name would be Jesus, the Savior of the world.

(Luke 1:28-35)

I told the angel that I accepted this responsibility. "Be it unto me according to thy word," I said. I was honored and humbled to be chosen to be the mother of Jesus.

(Luke 1:37-38)

Soon after that, I became pregnant, just as the angel said. After many months, while on a trip to Bethlehem, baby Jesus was born. Oh, how I remember that **special** night! I was so grateful I had **lived a virtuous life** and was worthy to receive this wonderful blessing.

(Luke 2:4-7, 19)

How can you LIVE A VIRTUOUS LIFE like Mary?

 "And ye must practice virtue and holiness before me continually."
—D&C 46:33

Living a virtuous life means **you treat your body like a temple.** You can do this by dressing modestly, avoiding inappropriate media, using clean language, and doing things that fill your life with the Holy Ghost.

Living a virtuous life means **you can be trusted.** You do what you say you're going to do. People can count on you. You are a promise keeper.

Living a virtuous life means **you love people.** You are a peacemaker. You are kind and always try to get along with others, especially your family.

Like Mary, your Father in Heaven has many wonderful blessings in store for you! Living a virtuous life helps you to **be worthy to receive all these blessings.**

81

MOM and DAD, this is section is for YOU! ☺

These **Family Home Evening Lesson Helps** are specifically designed to help you teach your children how the principles found within each story apply to them. I encourage you to use them! Take full advantage of these teaching tools and watch these scripture heroines come to life for your little ones.

A few notes on these FHE Lesson Helps:

CS = Children's Songbook (used in Primary)

LDS.org Children Videos = awesome, hand-picked Mormon Messages for Primary age kids! They are very easy to access and are listed alphabetically.

Go to lds.org / "Resources" (up top) – click on "Children" / click "Videos and Music" / click "Other Videos"

MtC = Make the Connection. These are the teaching moments that come after the activity.

Here are a few ACTIVITY ideas that can be used for <u>any</u> of these heroes:

WRITE A LETTER

Have each child write (or dictate) a letter to Eve, Rebekah, Esther, etc. . . . telling her how she has followed (or will follow) her heroic example. Next family home evening, deliver letters to the children that the heroine (aka Mom. Not Dad, his handwriting is terrible) has written back to them, commending them for their behavior.

YOU DRAW THE STORY

Read the "How Can You Be Like . . ." application pages for your featured heroine. Then, have each child draw her own application page of specific ways she can follow (or has recently followed) the heroine's example. Tuck the drawings into the book or put them on the refrigerator as reminders to always try to be like this scripture hero.

Also, Mom and Dad, FYI . . . as you go to the **"Resources— Children"** page at **lds.org,** you need to browse around and see <u>all</u> the FHE lesson helps you have there! A whole assortment of Videos and Music, Games and Activities, more sample lessons, the entire *Children's Songbook* and current Friend Magazine, and the "Resources for Teaching Children" section (so good!). Check it out!

And, while you are on **lds.org,** go to **"Resources—Youth"** and see all the materials available pertaining to the Young Women's Values (to help you teach each heroine's YW Value in this book). Oh, and there are 7 heroines in this book . . . 8 YW Values . . . Hhhmmm, which YW Value is missing? DIVINE NATURE. This is simply because ALL of them reflect this value! ☺

Good Luck with your Family Home Evenings!

Eve Makes the Best Choice
YW Value—Choice and Accountability

Hymn: "Choose the Right," #239

CS: "Choose the Right Way," p. 160

Scriptures: 2 Nephi 2:27 ; Alma 30:8; Helaman 14:30; D&C 37:4

LDS.org Children Video: "Continue in Patience"

Mormon Message: "Voice of the Spirit"

Friend **Article:** "Choose the Best" (February 2012 *Friend*)

"We have to forego some good things in order to choose others that are better or best because they develop faith in the Lord Jesus Christ." —Elder Dallin H. Oaks

ACTIVITIES:

FIRST THINGS FIRST

Display a jar, a cup of rocks, and a cup of sand. Tell the family their goal is to get all the rocks and all the sand to fit in the jar. First, have them try to do this by pouring the sand in FIRST, and then putting the rocks in SECOND. They won't all fit. Then have them try it the other way: put all the **rocks** in FIRST, and then pour the **sand** in second. The sand will trickle down between the rocks and both materials will all barely fit! (NOTE: You must do this experiment once ahead of time to make sure you have the right amount of rocks and sand to make this work for your size jar).

MtC: The jar = your life. The rocks = the "Best" choices like prayers, scripture study time, FHE, temple attendance (for mom and dad), service, etc. The sand = the "okay/not bad, but not

crucial" choices such as playing with friends, watching TV, social media, etc. When you prioritize by putting BEST things <u>first,</u> you are often able to still fit those other things into your life as well. The opposite is true when one focuses on the <u>not</u> crucial things first—Afterwards, there's seldom the time/motivation for the BEST choices.

FREE TO FLY

Each family member will make a paper airplane. (For the BEST/simplest paper airplane model I know . . . go to **http://www.wikihow.com/Make-a-Paper-Airplane** and scroll down to **"Method 2 of 3: Better Airplane"**). Each person folds his/her paper at the same time, in unison (older ones helping younger ones). With each fold, the family states out loud one "BEST" choice they can make in life (such as: daily prayer, happy obedience to parents, paying tithing, etc.) . . . until the plane is complete. Before you go outside and have a hey-day flying your planes, have this teaching moment:

MtC: The paper is our lives . . . blank. Each fold in the paper is a choice. When we follow prescribed patterns of living from prophets and scriptures (make the correct folds in the paper), we are using our agency to make choices that turn us into something useful (the paper airplane). If we don't follow any pattern in life and just choose whatever feels good at the moment (random folds that make no sense), then we won't be good for much.

Rebekah Loves Doing Good Works
YW Value—Good Works

Hymn: "Have I Done Any Good," #223

CS: "Go the Second Mile," p. 167

Scriptures: D&C 58:27 💡; Mosiah 2:17; Matthew 25:40; D&C 7:5

LDS.org Children Videos: "Dayton's Legs" / "Lessons I Learned As a Boy" / "Pass It On" / "The Coat" / "Unselfish Service"

***Friend* Article:** "Darren's Friend" (February 2012 *Friend*)

"This is the spirit of compassion: that we love others as ourselves, seek their happiness, and do unto them as we hope they would do unto us." —President Dieter F. Uchtdorf

ACTIVITIES:

CAMEL-LOT SERVICE

Each child traces their hand(s) on a separate sheet of paper. Next, they have fun decorating their hand to look like a camel (as shown) and cut them out. Since Rebekah gave all the camels a "hand" by giving them water, your family will have the chance to give each other a **"camel hand."** ☺ Throughout the next week, each family member thinks of a way to serve another family member, writes it down on the back of the camel,

and then does it, leaving behind their "camel hand" at the scene of the crime (service). The recipient of the "camel hand" then writes their own service idea on that camel they just received, does the service, and passes it on to someone else. This continues all week, "camel hands" changing hands with their good works inscribed on their backs each time, until they are all collected (and read out loud) at the next FHE.

MtC: At the next FHE, help them realize that when they are actively thinking about doing good works for others, they feel better inside.

Umm . . . HOW 'BOUT . . . DO SOME GOOD WORKS?

Actually do some service together FOR Family Home Evening (there's a new idea ☺). Bake/deliver cookies to someone you <u>prayerfully</u> decide needs the gesture of kindness the most. Visit a senior care facility and sing primary songs to them (they LOVE your little kiddos). Do yard work for a widow. The list goes on and on. Or . . . like it says in the AMMON story in my WYH vol. 1 . . .

BLITZ MOM!
For a specified amount of time, see how many "good deeds" the family can do for mom. Tidy up the house, do some dishes, clean rooms, sweep, dust, vacuum, massage Mom's feet . . . whatever she wants, as fast as you can! While she is being "blitzed" the only thing Mom is allowed to do is recline in a comfortable chair and breathe sighs of contentment. ☺ Aaahhhh.

Hannah Prays with Faith
YW Value—Faith

Hymn: "Did You Think to Pray," # 140

CS: "I Pray in Faith," p. 14

Scriptures: Ether 12:6 ; James 1:5–6; 2 Nephi 4:35; 3 Nephi 18:20

LDS.org Children Video: "A Mother's Hope"

Mormon Message: "Prayer"

Friend Articles: "A Patient Prayer" (June 2013 *Liahona* and *Friend*); "He Gives the Best Answers" (July 2013 *Friend*)

"We were not placed on this earth to walk alone. What an amazing source of power, of strength, and of comfort is available to each of us. He who knows us better than we know ourselves, He who sees the larger picture and who knows the end from the beginning, has assured us that He will be there for us to provide help if we but ask." —President Thomas S. Monson

ACTIVITIES:

One of the best explanations on this theme of "Praying with Faith" is found in the **Bible Dictionary—"Prayer," the paragraph that starts with "As soon as we learn the true relationship . . ."** Here are some fun little activities to help you teach the principles found in these Bible Dictionary paragraphs.

" . . . the true relationship in which we stand toward God (namely, God is our Father, and we are His children) . . ."

Matthew 7:7–11
These verses ("would a Dad give a snake to his child when he/she asked or a fish?") portray this concept perfectly. Dad, have your kids ask you for something . . . ANYTHING they might want? Then, give them something totally unrelated and not desirable

(like a wrapper, some dirt, hair shavings from your electric shaver, whatever! . . . have fun with it ☺)

MtC: A parent (earthly or heavenly) loves their children and wants the best for them! They <u>want</u> to answer their prayers and bless them with GOOD things! Read Matthew 7:7–11 with them.

"Prayer is the act by which the will of the Father and the will of the child are brought into correspondence with each other."

20 QUESTIONS
Mom or Dad thinks of a person or object from ANY scripture story. Kids ask only "yes or no" questions (up to 20 questions) to try to find out what it is. Play as many times as you'd like.

MtC: Explain to the children how it took a lot of effort for them to try to "align" their thoughts with Mom or Dad's thought. Thankfully, when we have the Holy Ghost with us, the things we naturally desire are usually the things Heavenly Father desires.

"Blessings require some work or effort on our part before we can obtain them. Prayer is a form of work"

PRAYER = WORK
With either a whiteboard, a poster board, or sheet(s) of paper, draw a line down the middle, making two columns. Title the 1st column - PRAYER. Title the 2nd second column - WORK. In the PRAYER column, ask kids "What is a blessing they/we might pray for?" Write it down. Then in WORK column, write the word "ask." But then ask the kids what MORE could they do to show the Lord how much they actually want this blessing. Make a list. Depending on the desired blessing, answers might include --- Pray multiple times about it, Fast for it, do things to help make it happen, live righteously, invite others to join your prayer, think about your desire throughout the day, show gratitude, be willing to accept it if it's not God's will, etc.

Sariah Obeys the Lord Willingly
YW Value—Individual Worth

Hymn: "Keep the Commandments," #303

CS: "Nephi's Courage," p. 120

Scriptures: Proverbs 3:5–6 ; Abraham 3:25; Alma 57:21; D&C 58:29

LDS.org Children Video: "Continue in Patience"

Friend **Article:** "Now Is the Time to Obey" (August 2008 *Friend*)

"Jesus taught us to obey in simple language that is easy to understand: 'If ye love me, keep my commandments,' and 'Come, follow me'." —Elder Robert D. Hales

ACTIVITIES:

MOTHER, WANT I?

This is the classic "Mother, may I?" game (one of the versions, at least), but with a twist.

First, play the game normally. Mom stands facing away from the line of kids. She then chooses a child (at random, or in order), and announces a direction. These follow a pattern, such as, "Sarah, you may take' x' giant/regular/baby steps forward/backward." The child responds with "Mother, may I?" Mom then states "Yes" or "No", depending on her whim, and the child complies. If the child forgets to ask "Mother may I?" he/she goes back to the starting line. First one to touch Mother wins.

THEN, play the game again but change the response to **"Mother, WANT I?"** Then, whether Mom says "yes" or "no" . . . it doesn't matter, **the child does the action anyway.** If they <u>don't</u> do the action (or if they forget to ask "Mother, WANT I?" like the original game), they go back to start.

MtC: When the Lord (or your parents for that matter) asks you to do something, it is irrelevant whether or not you WANT to do it. You obey regardless.

OBEY WHICH WAY?

Give each child a handful of some small object (I like cheerios because they are "O" shaped. "O" for "Obedience"). On the floor, lay down one big SMILEY face ☺ . . . and one big FROWNY face ☹ that you or the kids drew. Then, come up with a variety of scenarios (involving God's commandments or parental instructions) where children can choose to either **OBEY HAPPILY, OBEY w/WHINING** or **DISOBEY.** Single out one child at a time, give him/her the scenario, and then have him/her roll a dice to see their response. If it's a:

> **1 or 2 — they OBEY HAPPILY**
>
> **3 or 4 — they OBEY w/WHINING**
>
> **5 or 6 — they DISOBEY**

Then, depending on their rolled response, ask the child to place one "cheerio" on the face that best represents how they would FEEL **after** they had that kind of response.

MtC: After you're finished, help them make the connection that whether they DISOBEYED or OBEYED w/WHINING **. . . it had the same effect on how they felt.** Willing or cheerful obedience is really the ONLY option that brings happiness/blessings.

Esther Stands Up for the Right
YW Value—Integrity

Hymn: "True to the Faith," #254

CS: "Dare to Do Right," p. 158

Scriptures: Philippians 4:13 ; Mosiah 18:9; D&C 27:15; Romans 1:16

LDS.org Children Video: "Dare to Stand Alone"

Mormon Message: "Courage"

***Friend* Articles:** "The Bad Movie" (June 2013 *Liahona* and *Friend*); "Andy's Choice" (May 2008 *Friend*)

"Let us have the courage to stand for principle [what is right]. Courage, not compromise, brings the smile of God's approval. A moral coward is one who is afraid to do what he thinks is right because others will disapprove or laugh." —President Thomas S. Monson

ACTIVITIES:

TIME TO STAND!
(Two fun, little "stand up" activities to get the blood flowing ☺)

• Play "Duck, Duck, GOOSE!" . . . but replace the words with "wrong, wrong, RIGHT!"

MtC: Explain how we **never** stand up for the Wrong ☹ . . . and we **never** **hesitate** to stand up for the **RIGHT** ☺. Silly, I know . . . but, hey, these are kids ☺.

• Have family members sit on the floor, back-to-back, and try to stand up using only the pressure from the other person's back (no arms). After successfully doing it in pairs, try it in groups of 3, 4, 5, etc.

MtC: It helps to have the support of other people when you "stand up" for the right in a difficult situation, just like Esther had from Mordecai, the Jews, and especially from the Holy Ghost.

A RECTANGLE IS A RECTANGLE
Draw four shapes on four sheets of paper (one on each sheet). A circle, a square, a triangle, and a rectangle. Place them on the floor and ask the children if they can identify the shapes and give each one the chance to do so. Then, point to the rectangle and ask "What if I were to say this is an <u>oval</u>, <u>not</u> a rectangle? Would that change your mind of what it is?" Continue with questions like "What if your best friend said it was an oval? What if your whole class at school called it an oval? etc. Would that change your mind?" Ask them to explain WHY it wouldn't make a difference what other people called it . . . it would **still** be a rectangle!

MtC: Help them come to the conclusion that truth is truth, regardless of how many people say it is something else. In today's world, media, other people, etc. might say that something is perfectly okay, . . .when we, as LDS, know that it goes against God's truth. We must have the courage, like Esther, to stand up for the truth in these situations. Don't be persuaded by popular opinion or peer pressure.

Finish by reciting together the well-known adage found in Pres. Monson's "Dare to Stand Alone" video:

Dare to be a Mormon, Dare to stand alone,
Dare to have a purpose firm, Dare to make it known.

Hymn: "The Lord is My Light," # 89

CS: "The Holy Ghost," p. 105

Scriptures: D&C 8:2-3 ; Moroni 7:13; D&C 85:6; 1 Nephi 4:6

LDS.org Children Videos: "Activity Day Rescuers" / "195 Dresses"

Mormon Message: "Voice of the Spirit"

***Friend* Article:** "Spiritual Promptings" (February 2012 *Friend*)

"One who is obedient to His commandments is trusted of the Lord. That individual has access to His inspiration to know what to do and, as needed, the divine power to do it." —Elder Richard G. Scott

ACTIVITIES:

CLINKING THINKING

Put a marble in a jar and have a child shake it. Point out the repetitive "clinking sound" of the marble bouncing around. Next, add a cotton ball to the jar and shake again. A little less clinking noise. Then add another cotton ball, less clinking still. Keep adding cotton balls until you can barely/no longer hear the marble at all.

MtC: The marble is a spiritual prompting (or inspiration) from the Holy Ghost. When our thoughts are clear and uncluttered from distractions (cotton balls), we notice the clinking marble sound (the Holy Ghost communicating with us) easily. But when we start to crowd out minds with distractions, sin, etc. (adding the cotton balls), little by little we stop noticing the promptings

of the Spirit in our lives, even though the spirit is still trying to communicate with you. We become desensitized. Have children list what some of these distractions are (like video games, the variety of media out there, arguments, etc.)

SPIRIT GUIDES

Spread a whole bunch of stuffed animals (or some other safe items) on the floor with a prize at the end of the room. One at a time, blindfold each child at the other end of the room and have him/her try to walk to the prize without stepping on a stuffed animal. When they have a hard time doing it, ask them if they would like a guide. Then, have each child try it again blindfolded, but this time with Mom or Dad whispering directions to them (or for younger kids, physically helping them through the maze).

MtC: Have children share all the ways how this activity is like following the promptings of the Holy Ghost. Some possible ideas—The Holy Ghost shows us where to go to be happy. He steers us away from things that are harmful (spiritually or even physically). It is a quiet whisper. We still have to choose to listen and walk the steps (HG doesn't walk for us).

ONE MORE THING . . .

Be sure to emphasize that the Holy Ghost almost always gives us promptings in FIRST PERSON! Meaning, instead of hearing some outside voice that says "Rachel, you need to do (this)" or "Sarah, don't do (that)" . . . you will get a THOUGHT or an IDEA (not a voice, necessarily) that will feel like "Hhhhmm, maybe **I** need to go do (this)" or "Boy, **I** better not do (that)." To support this, point out in the Abish story how it says ***"This gave me an idea . . ."*** and also note how the spirit's prompting is worded on page 8 of the Eve story.

Mary Lives a Virtuous Life
YW Value—Virtue

Hymn: "Teach Me to Walk," #304

CS: "I'm Trying to Be like Jesus," p. 78

Scriptures: D&C 46:33 ; D&C 121:45; D&C 25:2; Proverbs 31:10

LDS.org Children's Video: "Deep Beauty"

Mormon Message: "Return to Virtue"

Friend Article: "The Orange Shirt" (May 2013 *Friend*)

"There is no more beautiful sight than a young woman who glows with the light of the Spirit, who is confident and courageous because she is virtuous." —Sister Elaine Dalton

ACTIVITIES:

LIGHT IT UP!

Give each child a pencil and a sheet of paper. Tell them you are going to give them step-by-step instructions on a scene for them to draw. Before you do, though, turn out all the lights and have them look at the ceiling . . . so there's no way for them to actually SEE what they are about to draw. Then proceed to tell them each item to draw. Start with "Draw the outline of a house in the middle of the paper." Then instruct, "Draw a tree next to the house." Then, "Draw a fence on the other side of the house." Then, "Some clouds." Then say, "Oh, I forgot! Put a door and a window on the house" (this always flusters 'em ☺). Then keep mentioning other items, like mailbox, the sun, smoke coming out of the chimney, a bush, a smiley face IN the sun ☺, a kid sticking his head out the house's window and waving, etc. When they are all finished, turn on the lights and have a good laugh at these crazy drawings.

MtC: Living a virtuous life is like having light in your life. It helps you see clearly the things you need to do. Without virtue lighting up your life, it's impossible to do your best work (just like this drawing). Ask them "What kind of things do we do to help us feel light/virtue in their lives?"

SOAK IT UP!

In the kitchen, prepare shallow bowls filled with following substances: clean water, really dirty water, milk, juice/kool-aid (something colorful), etc. Bring the family in and have each child choose a bowl. Then, give each of the children a sponge (or you can use the same sponge and just rinse it out). Have them soak their sponge(s) in their respective bowls until the liquid is completely absorbed. Then announce, "Okay, it's time to wash our hands for our FHE treat! Bring your sponges to the sink!" Have them hold their hands over the sink and one at a time, squeeze the liquid out of their respective sponges over their hands. When finished, ask them "Whose hands feel clean & ready to be used for eating?" When they protest that they're hands aren't clean . . . help <u>them</u> make the connection:

MtC: The sponges are us. Our minds and spirits are always "soaking up" the influences around us, whether they be good, clean influences (the pure water) or not-so-good influences (the other liquids). Have the kids list what some of these good and bad influences might be. Explain that "Once we soak up these influences inside us, then we naturally exude (there's a good word ☺) these same influences back out." Garbage in, Garbage out (as my Jr. High English teacher would always say). In addition, teach them that when we do make mistakes and choose poor influences, fortunately . . . we have a Savior who made it possible for use to be repent and be cleansed. Then, offer them the soap (repentance) so they can go back to the sink and wash off the sticky juice, milk, etc. and thus, feel clean (worthy) when they eat the FHE treat.

About the Author/Illustrator

Following his service as a full-time missionary in the Philippines, David Bowman graduated with a degree in illustration from Brigham Young University. He has since served as a release-time seminary instructor as well as a counselor and speaker at numerous EFY conferences. His special love is making the scriptures come to life for young people.

David is the author/illustrator of the bestselling *Who's Your Hero? Book of Mormon Stories Applied to Children* series. His other books include *The Great Plan of Happiness; Dude, Don't Be a Lemuel: A Teenage Guide to Avoiding Lemuelitis;* and *What Would the Founding Fathers Think? A YOUNG Americans Guide to Understanding What Makes Our Nation Great and How We've Strayed.*

He and his wife, Natalie, and their five children live in Arizona.

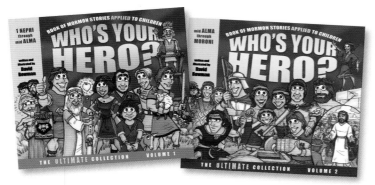

For more Who's Your Hero? fun stuff, products, bonus material, etc. go to
www.whosyourherobooks.com

David Bowman is also the artist of the "Expressions of Christ" series. You can see his fine-art depictions of the Savior, as well as his other books, at
www.davidbowmanart.com